A unique wagon – in the United Kingdom. In 1999, the completely overhauled boiler of Ipswich-built Ransomes, Sims & Jefferies wagon No. 34270, a type SW 8/1 dating from September 1923, came back from Australia and the rest of the wagon has been reconstructed by an enthusiast in South Wales. It was one of only thirty-three examples built by the firm and was originally supplied to Ruston & Hornsby of Melbourne without a body but with three-way hydraulic tipping gear. Coincidentally, the boiler was actually made by Ruston in Lincoln and looked very much like a stayless Robey pistol-type boiler. The completed vehicle made its rally debut in mid 2002 and is pictured by Paul Stratford at the Welland Rally.

Steam Wagons

Derek Rayner

A Shire book

Published in 2003 by Shire Publications Ltd,
Cromwell House, Church Street, Princes Risborough,
Buckinghamshire HP27 9AA, UK.
(Website: www.shirebooks.co.uk)

British Library Cataloguing in Publication Data:
Rayner, Derek.
Steam wagons. – (Shire album; 413)
1. Steam-engines 2. Trucks
I. Title 629.2'292
ISBN 0 7478 0551 2

Dedicated to the late Tom Varley, whose personal devotion to the acquisition of rare and unique steam wagons – sometimes from far and distant lands – and their subsequent restoration has left British steam road enthusiasts a lasting legacy of which they can be proud. Without Tom's unselfish dedication to this self-imposed but nevertheless enjoyable task, we would have been all the poorer.

Cover: *5 ton Clayton & Shuttleworth steam wagon No. 47838 was built in Lincoln in 1916. It was exported to Australia – to agents Dalgety & Co, Sydney – and was last used in the Corowa district of New South Wales in 1959. Usually fired on wood, it is owned and was restored by John Norris. It is pictured on display in May 2002 at the seventy-ninth twice-yearly Lake Goldsmith Steam Rally in Victoria. This is the earliest of only five wagons known to exist world-wide from this manufacturer.*

ACKNOWLEDGEMENTS
The illustrations are by the author or from the author's collection – unless stated otherwise. He wishes to acknowledge the valuable assistance of the Road Locomotive Society, the Leeds & District Traction Engine Club and others named in regard to the provision of some of the photographs and also their help in captioning them. Thanks also to others who have provided specific information from their archive records.
In addition, it should perhaps be mentioned that one early steam wagon building firm was located at Rayleigh in Essex. It was known as the Standard Steam Lorry & Wagon Co and was taken over in 1907 by one Thomas James Rayner – who then lived in Victoria Avenue, Southend. He renamed the business T. J. Rayner & Sons. The author had distant relations at one time in Coggeshall, Essex, and although circumstances have not yet permitted family history research to confirm a connection – or otherwise – it is interesting to speculate whether a tenuous link does exist between the two family names and whether this might account for the author's very keen interest in all types of steam road vehicles!

Printed in Great Britain by CIT Printing Services Ltd, Press Buildings, Merlins Bridge, Haverfordwest, Pembrokeshire SA61 1XF

Contents

An unusual load for Foden steam wagon No. 6666. Taken in France, the photograph depicts W. Woodhead as the driver, who later worked for a Leeds firm of haulage contractors. The load is a captured German railway locomotive. It is understood that the wagon was eventually returned to England and was one of several former War Department wagons bought by Yorkshire's North Riding County Council, which used it as a platform wagon for some years afterwards. (Photograph: L&DTEC collection)

A line-up of four very early Leeds-built steam wagons – all undertypes – at Bentley's Yorkshire Brewery's Eshaldwell Brewery, Woodlesford, Leeds, in the early years of the twentieth century. From the right: 4 ton Yorkshire No. 56 of 1904; 2½ ton Yorkshire No. 80 of 1905; two unidentified Mann's wagons – a 5 tonner belonging to the brewery and another smaller model – dating from around 1904 and 1901 respectively. The brewery had its own sidings connected to the Midland Railway and the last wagon is believed to have been owned by the East & West Yorkshire Union Railway and was used for transporting beer to that railway's base at Rothwell, about 3 miles (5 km) away, for shipment to Great Northern Railway destinations and beyond.

The early years

The first recorded steam road vehicle was built by a Frenchman, Nicholas Cugnot, in 1769 for military use – as a gun tractor – but it was a very crude machine. Steam engines were developed in Britain in the latter years of the eighteenth century from the requirement of pumping water out of mine shafts. Railway uses followed in the early nineteenth century; Trevithick, Murray and Stephenson were in their own ways all pioneers in bringing serviceable steam locomotives to the ever increasing railway track mileage and, with them, they created and speeded up the public transport of the time.

In the 1830s, steam carriages built by such people as Gurney and Hancock travelled around the roads carrying passengers, but up to the mid nineteenth century the use of steam power to carry a commercial load on the conveyance itself had apparently not been thought of or put into practice. Traction engines that pulled their load behind on a trailer had been developed – the first of which, a very light machine known as the *Farmer's Friend*, dated from 1849. This was followed by Thomas Aveling's major step forward in 1859 of creating a self-moving machine using a portable engine – by fitting a long drive-chain between its crankshaft and rear axle. Further details of such road steam vehicles are given in other Shire Albums.

An early version of a Robey steam wagon with a vertical boiler and underslung engine, one cylinder of which can be seen below the chassis, almost under the driver's seat. This is a Robey official photograph showing it in Great Central Railway livery in around 1906. There were several similar wagons listed to this owner but details in existence do not allow this one to be positively identified.

A report in the Yorkshire newspaper the *Huddersfield Chronicle*, dated 5th May 1860 and entitled 'A Steam Horse', concerns a vehicle described as a 'steam traction engine', which the founder of a local boilermaking firm, William Arnold, had had built for transporting his boilers to customers. The technical description of this boiler-carrying wagon indicated that the machine's engine and boiler were constructed on the ordinary locomotive principle; the frame was made of wrought iron, 32 feet (9.75 metres) in length and over 8 feet (2.44 metres) wide, and it was said that the wagon could convey a load of 60 tons. There were four wheels, 4 feet (1.22 metres) in diameter and 14 inches (356 mm) broad, and these contained 'slight indentations for the purpose of causing them to bite into soft roads'. The guiding wheels were worked by means of a lever, pinion and quadrant.

Unfortunately, an illustration of this early boiler-carrying steam wagon does not appear to have survived. Other better chronicled and somewhat similar 'wagons' were produced by John Yule, Glasgow, in 1870; Brown & May of Devizes in 1875; James Sumner, Leyland, in 1884; Phoenix, Bolton, in 1888; and Elliott & Garood of Beccles in 1890.

Such transport fell foul of the notorious 1865 'Red Flag' Act, which stated that all mechanically propelled vehicles had to have a man walking in front. Although the carrying of a red flag was rescinded in 1876, until this disastrous Act was fully repealed in 1896 the development of better transportation for both people and goods on the roads in Britain was heavily restricted. After 1896, things improved considerably.

The Liverpool Self-propelled Traffic Association organised a series of Heavy Motor Car trials in 1898, 1899 and 1901, which gave these new styles of vehicle a suitable opportunity at which to be demonstrated. The first such recorded steam-propelled commercial vehicle of this era was actually an oil-fired van – Thornycroft No. 1 – which had been built in Chiswick, London, in 1896 and which still

There are only two surviving examples of wagons by Thornycroft in the United Kingdom; this one is in Lincolnshire and is No. 39 of 1900 – from an era when production of such vehicles was in its infancy. It is a very fortunate survivor.

exists. This was made by a firm which, at that time, was involved in relatively small water-borne steam craft. It was thus only a very small step to position such a marine steam plant on to a 'cart' and to make a self-propelled goods vehicle. Traction engines and the like had then been around for more than half a century and were very good at towing things, but to carry goods on the chassis of a self-propelled vehicle was believed to be a revolutionary concept – despite its having been invented some thirty years previously – and it consequently became very much *the* way forward for the speedy transportation of goods.

The interesting thing with the initial trials in Liverpool was that from around fifty invitations issued to prospective participants only three firms turned up, despite the incentive of a gold medal for the winner. Internal combustion engines of the time were not sufficiently developed to be able to haul a weight of 2 tons around the course – the judge's requirements as set out in the competition's rules – and so it was only steam wagons that participated.

A Clarkson steam wagon, loaded high with what appear to be sacks of coke: an interesting and unusual type of vehicle, which used coke as fuel. A chassis of a similar vehicle is known to exist in Australia.

Restored as an example of an early Mann's overtype wagon, this machine had been converted from a steam cart to a roller and was used commercially as such by Isaac Ball, an agricultural and road-rolling contractor from Wharles, near Blackpool, Lancashire. Pictured at Harrogate in 1994, it is the earliest operable example from this maker in the United Kingdom, being No. 881 of 1914.

For the first trial, the three competitors were the Lancashire Steam Motor Company from Leyland, Lancashire, Thornycroft and Lifu, a company from the Isle of Wight. Lifu is an acronym for Liquid Fuel, for this company's wagon burned kerosene or paraffin. Success in the initial trial came to the Leyland-produced vehicle, which won a prize of £100. Rather surprisingly, three years later at the final trial there had still not been much progress with internal combustion engined vehicles. On this occasion, eight competitors entered thirteen vehicles between them, of which eight were steam driven. As a result, gold medals were awarded to Leyland, Thornycroft and Coulthard, with Mann's receiving a silver medal.

Many traction engines and their derivatives were constructed throughout England. Only a few were built in Scotland and none came from Wales or Ireland. The two cities of Leeds and Lincoln and the largely agricultural areas of East Anglia and Hampshire feature very prominently as locations for traction engine building but none was produced in the industrial heartlands of Birmingham, the Black Country or Manchester. This was not the case, however, with steam wagons. While most established traction engine manufacturers took up the construction of such vehicles, not all were drawn into the fold. Well-known makers who made both include Allchin; Fowler; Mann's; Aveling & Porter; Foden; Clayton & Shuttleworth; Foster; Burrell; Wallis & Steevens; Tasker; Robey; Ransomes, Sims & Jefferies;

Savage of King's Lynn built this OA type wagon for the Leicester Corporation in 1905. It would have been used for road watering to slake the dust that was very prevalent on water-bound roads before the advent of tarred surfaces. (Photograph courtesy of John Middlemiss)

The Sheppee Motor Company of York made this liquid-fired steam wagon in 1913 and it worked locally for the Tadcaster Tower Brewery Co Ltd. The firm also made vehicles with interchangeable bodies – in one mode a wagon, in the other a charabanc. At least one wagon, which it termed its 'Overseas Special', was exported – to South America. Since no records of the firm from that period have survived, the exact production numbers are not known.

Garrett; and Savage. However, still remaining on the outside were others such as Marshall, McLaren, Ruston and Green.

There were other firms that built nothing but wagons (in the road sense) – such as Atkinson, Thornycroft and Leyland, as well as Sentinel and Yorkshire. The last two also had excursions into the railway field at one time or another – with, in the case of Sentinel, some considerable degree of success.

In the early years of the twentieth century, in the development of the goods-carrying steam wagon, there was a plethora of small firms that designed and built these vehicles. Many of them quickly fell by the wayside, although some firms continued quite successfully in other directions for many more years – Sheppee of York, Carter of Rochdale and Beyer Peacock of Manchester are in this latter category. Gone without

Above: After a great deal of searching, this Leyland steam wagon was found and brought back by the firm from Australia in a very poor condition in the late 1960s. After extensive restoration by Leyland apprentices, it appeared at the conclusion of the Trans-Pennine Commercial Vehicle Run in Harrogate, North Yorkshire, in 1970. Although the design is very reminiscent of the firm's early products, this unidentified wagon is thought to date from around 1923.

Right: One of the late Tom Varley's restorations was a small 2 ton Yorkshire wagon, the chassis of which had finished up as a farm cart in North Wales. Its early history was traced through the local Archive Office records, it being No. 117 and dating from 1905. Considerable restoration work eventually turned it into the splendid vehicle pictured here by Dave McNamee at Slaidburn, Lancashire, in May 2002 in a later ownership and by then named 'Denby Maiden'.

Left: *The North Eastern Railway (NER) at York was an early user of steam wagons on a collection and delivery service that it instituted from various goods stations. The railway tried at least five different maker's versions, including this St Pancras wagon, built at the Holloway Ironworks in London in 1905. It is posed by the Railway Offices in York, outside the NER No. 1 Fire Brigade Station, which was located where the Railway War Memorial now stands. York city walls are in the background. It was presumably photographed when very new since there is an untypical lack of lettering to indicate ownership of the vehicle. (Photograph courtesy of Ken Hoole)*

Right: *The first steam wagons tried by the North Eastern Railway were a pair of Strakers in 1904 and they must have been satisfactory since another five were purchased soon afterwards. This is fleet No. 1 – with a traction wagon in tow – at Tollerton, 12 miles (19 km) north of York, where the first collection and delivery service to Brandsby commenced in October 1904. The tree is still recognisable a century or so later. The photograph is dated 1st November 1904. The registration mark (A.4.S) is an early form of trade plate, which was allocated to Strakers, presumably for wagon delivery purposes. Despite extensive research, the first local registration carried by the wagon has not been positively identified – although one of this pair was registered DN 3 on 6th February 1906 – after it had been in service for some fifteen months. (Photograph courtesy of Bill McDonald)*

trace in the wagon-building line, however, are such firms as Standard, Ellis, Musker, Belhaven, St Pancras, Londonderry, Robertson, Pratchett, Straker, Nayler and Toward.

Other British firms imported similar ideas from abroad and set up agencies for foreign manufacturers in Great Britain. Dougill of Leeds was one – it marketed German-built Hagen steam wagons for a time in around 1900 – and there were also others that imported wagons from Purrey in France and Buffalo-Springfield in the United States, examples of which worked in the London area at one time.

A Leeds-built steam cart by Mann's Patent Steam Cart and Wagon Company, at work in Leeds. This was owned by the Leeds Forge Co Ltd and is No. 1070 of 1913. (Photograph courtesy of S. Bottomley)

9

Typical steam wagon configurations

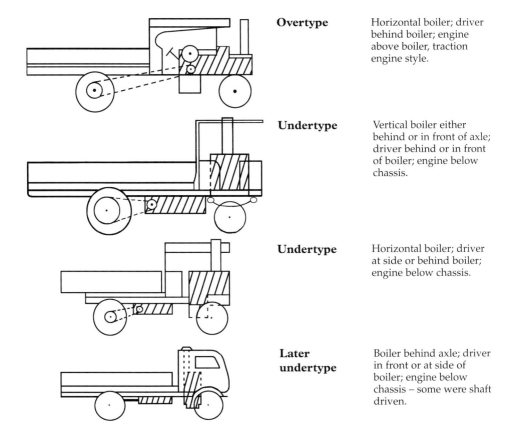

Overtype
Horizontal boiler; driver behind boiler; engine above boiler, traction engine style.

Undertype
Vertical boiler either behind or in front of axle; driver behind or in front of boiler; engine below chassis.

Undertype
Horizontal boiler; driver at side or behind boiler; engine below chassis.

Later undertype
Boiler behind axle; driver in front or at side of boiler; engine below chassis – some were shaft driven.

Note: in these diagrams, the position of the boiler and engine is indicated by hatching.

There were several other steam wagon variations not covered above. For example, one early type used front-wheel drive; on another, the boiler and engine were carried on a sub-frame, and, on yet another, two engines were mounted behind the rear axle. The Yorkshire wagon had a transverse double-ended boiler with a vertical engine either behind or at the side of the driver and the Fowler utilised a vertical boiler with a 'vee' type engine beneath the driver.

Power transmission was usually by chain drive on early wagons but Fowler's and later designs of wagons by Mann's, Sentinel, Foden and Yorkshire were shaft driven.

Overtype wagons

In the early years of the twentieth century, several ideas were promulgated as to what was the best layout for a steam wagon. Perhaps not surprisingly, traction engine makers took to wagon construction very easily. What they were already building in the form of a traction engine or a steam roller – where the propulsion unit is generally mounted above the boiler – was relatively easily adapted into wagon form by the addition of long chassis members and a body on the back. Well-known makers of this type included firms such as Aveling & Porter, Burrell, Robey, Clayton & Shuttleworth, Wallis & Steevens, Tasker, Foden and Mann's.

One of the first in this field was Foden, which caused some problems for those that followed since this firm patented its design of wagon frame in 1901 – and some of the other firms fell foul of this, resulting in expensive litigation and a design modification by the losers to circumnavigate the patented design.

There was plenty of competition in the market place. In 1911 Sentinel, which until then had made only undertype wagons, produced an overtype wagon – making a further sixteen – but the design was not a success and perhaps proved to the firm that its own way was the best – a situation ultimately rewarded by the number of 'copies' made of the original Sentinel style of vehicle in the 1920s and the fact that this company was the last manufacturer of steam wagons.

Allchin's first wagon was made in 1910 and its last in 1931, over 250 vehicles being made during that

Right: Foden wagon No. 6368 of 1916 used to belong to the maker and was shown at many events by Foden in the past. It is now part of the National Museum of Science and Industry transport collection and is in store at Wroughton, Wiltshire, where it can be seen on open days or by prior arrangement.

Drinks manufacturers found Foden wagons a very useful vehicle for conveying their products. The Great Dorset Steam Fair in 1988 was an interesting setting for this example, pictured in the livery of a cider maker. It is Foden No. 13316 of 1929.

11

In company with an ex-British Rail Scammell Scarab and a Sentinel Super wagon, 1929 Foden wagon No. 13476 is photographed at the weighbridge at the National Railway Museum in York.

time. Some of the early ones were fired from the side, in a manner similar to that adopted almost as standard by Mann's. Aveling & Porter had a somewhat shorter time span, starting in 1909 and concluding its output of almost three hundred wagons in 1925.

Burrell started in 1910 and was perhaps not as successful as its contemporaries, having made only just over 110 when the last was built in 1928. Unfortunately none has survived in its entirety, although one is being rebuilt in the south of England.

Foden at Sandbach, Cheshire, having first experimented in 1899, was one of the firms that very successfully made a wagon in the shape of its existing products and continued with this principle virtually

Aveling & Porter steam wagon No. 8546 of 1915 (KT 4852) was owned by the Taroads Syndicate Ltd of London, which had many such wagons on road surfacing jobs all over Britain. The large tank on the rear could be filled from rail tankers by means of the pump on the side of the wagon. The tar in the tank was kept hot by an internal steam coil and a spray-bar was fitted at the bottom rear with jets to direct the hot liquid on to the road surface. A gritter came along afterwards to spread fine grit on top of the tar and this was then rolled by a following steam roller. (Photograph courtesy of M. Thackrah)

The Bass Museum in Burton upon Trent, Staffordshire, was an ideal location for the owner of 1928 Foden wagon No. 13120 to display his vehicle in its brewery livery. The wagon may not have carried a tank in its commercial days, but on a rally field the provision of water to other engines using such a method is a boon to the event organisers.

Foden wagon No. 3510 had only recently returned from a long sojourn in the United States when this photograph was taken in 1987 at the Black Country Museum at Dudley, West Midlands. It had been on display at the Henry Ford Museum at Dearborn, Michigan, and the condition of its original paintwork brought forth appreciative comments from many enthusiasts. This has subsequently been treated so that it can be retained in this condition as a fine example of original 1913 signwriter's art. The furniture remover's box van body is typical of the wagon's use in that period.

Many Foden wagons were used in France on supply duties during the First World War. Three of these wagons in Army use with their WD lettering feature on a French-produced postcard that was sent by 'Steve' to his friend Mr W. Ingram in Leicester. See also the Foden at the top of page 14 regarding 'buffers'.

Left: *A great number of steam wagons saw service during the First World War carrying general supplies for the troops. This example of a Foden with a tipping body is No. 7768 of 1917 and still retains its army livery. It was found in France many years after the war had finished and was brought back to England, where it was restored. An interesting addition, which was kept, was the two small protrusions (buffers) on the front of the machine. These were provided for pushing broken-down wagons when necessary.*

Right: *Foden tractor No. 13218 of 1929 takes to the rally arena at Masham, North Yorkshire. This example was cut down from a wagon and is seen in the guise of a haulage tractor – which the Sandbach firm supplied in large quantities to estates for timber haulage and such like.*

Left: *Over a period of some twelve years, the firm of Robert Brett & Sons, haulage contractors and quarry owners, of Canterbury, Kent, bought some twenty-three Foden steam wagons. Many of these were second-hand but the firm purchased seven new models in 1928/9 and presumably this staged photograph was organised for publicity purposes as a result of this investment. There are at least nine of the Cheshire firm's products visible, together with several petrol lorries. (Photograph: N. J. Tilly collection)*

Right: *Showmen used some steam wagons in the course of their activities and decorated them with the usual trappings of their business, such as twisted brass canopy supports and a dynamo. This 'D' Type tractor, new in 1926, is presumed to be pictured at Foden's works in around 1929 after conversion and before delivery to Simons & Greatorex, amusement caterers of Nantwich, Cheshire, to whom it was sold second-hand. In this firm's ownership it received the name 'Little John' and is Foden No. 12372 (NR 9505). Surprisingly, it remained somewhat plainly decorated compared with other similar wagons. (Photograph: L&DTEC collection)*

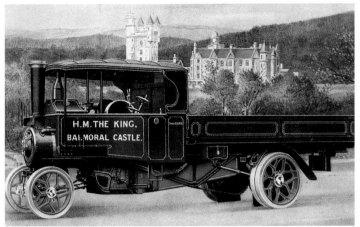

right to the end. Many vehicles were supplied as shortened haulage tractors and one lorry even had a bus body fitted to carry the Foden Works Band. It was only the intense competition from other makers that caused Foden to produce an undertype wagon in its latter days of production. The last overtype was produced in 1934, this being a tractor for South Africa. In total, this firm made around 6,500 steam wagons and tractors.

Robey of Lincoln commenced with undertype wagons but by 1914 had decided to concentrate on overtypes and by the end of the First World War had designed a stay-less pistol-type boiler, which also saw use as the basis for Robey's tandem steam rollers. Around 260 wagons were made between 1914 and 1934, several of which were exported, but many were also bought by road contractors and other firms in Britain. In the same city, Foster started with a prototype in 1905 and in the years up to 1933 produced only around sixty wagons, just one of which survives. Also in Lincoln, Clayton & Shuttleworth and later, after 1920, Clayton Wagons made around 1,300 until going into

A splendid photograph of a Robey overtype wagon owned by Thomas & Evans & John Dyer Ltd of Llanelli, Carmarthenshire. This was one of a pair that the firm owned but it is unclear which one this Robey official photograph depicts.

15

The sole surviving Foster wagon was restored to working order by Tom Varley after he had bought it in Australia and returned it to its country of origin. It is No. 14470, built in Lincoln in 1921, and now carries an 'age-related' registration number. It is named 'Tritton' after William Tritton – one of the principals of the firm. It was photographed by Andy Robson at Kirkby Stephen, Cumbria, in 2002.

Right: *Clayton & Shuttleworth 5 ton overtype wagon No. 45554 of 1913. Priddy, Stanley & Co were engineers and haulage contractors in the South Yorkshire village of Oughtibridge and the First World War may well have had some considerable impact on the firm's business since this was the only steam vehicle registered to them and it went back to the makers in 1915. (Photograph: Peter Smart collection)*

liquidation in 1930. Some of these wagons were made with a special flanged smokebox so they could be converted, by the addition of various components, into a steam roller – and others were supplied with twisted brass and a front-mounted dynamo for showground use.

Between 1909 and 1927 Garrett made almost seven hundred overtype wagons while at the same time also making undertypes. The sizes were 3 ton to 6 ton and one major technical variation was that all the 3 tonners were fitted with superheaters in an attempt to improve their efficiency, and several of the larger sizes also had this feature. This was unusual for a locomotive-type boiler on a road vehicle. Only one example remains intact, in Canada. Another Suffolk

The Garrett overtype wagon was first produced in 1908. This example, a superheated model, was owned by the Doncaster firm of Thomas Hanley & Sons Ltd of Low Fishergate, flour millers. The firm sold it in 1915 to Ernest Warriner, manure merchants of Sheffield. It is No. 30247 of 1912 and is a 3 ton model.

16

A unique survivor is this 6 ton three-way tipper Garrett overtype wagon, which was exported to Canada for preservation in the 1950s. It is No. 34932 and was made in 1926; the Leiston firm made around a thousand wagons between 1904 and 1931. Registered SX 2395, this example was used commercially by William Aitken of Stockbridge, Scotland, before being returned to Garrett, which firm sold it on to Devon County Council in 1927. (Photograph courtesy of R. A. Whitehead)

maker was Ransomes, Sims & Jefferies, which was relatively late on the scene for a noted traction engine manufacturer. This firm made its first wagon in 1920 and produced only around thirty-five in total up to 1930. One remarkable vehicle was a 10 ton articulated six-wheeler.

Mann's of Leeds made not only wagons but also a variation on the same theme in the form of a steam cart, with a tipping back, which was first produced in 1898. In addition, this firm made small patching rollers that could carry road-making materials within the body at the rear. With the cessation of Mann's activities in 1928, records were destroyed and it is thus not known how many vehicles in total were produced. The firm had dramatically redesigned its wagons in 1924 and introduced the 'Express' undertype range, coming, as indeed did Foden, almost to mirror the style of Sentinel, but it was by then too late as the oil-engine brigade was winning the battle and eventually won the war.

An example of a Mann's Patent Steam Cart and Wagon Co steam tractor, which was built in the latter years of the company in 1928; it is No. 1747. This design was based on a wagon but was much shorter in length. It is part of the Open Air Museum's display at Beamish in County Durham and can often be seen there in steam on summer weekends. The crew discuss their next foray into the busy visitor area.

Milestones museum at Basingstoke was opened in late 2000 and one of its features is a display stand, like those used by traction engine and steam wagon makers at agricultural shows and similar events in the past. One of the steam wagons in the Hampshire County Museums Service (HCMS) collection is the only surviving Tasker 'Little Giant' wagon. This was restored 'in house' and is a credit to the HCMS. It was built in Andover, Hampshire, and is No. 1915 of 1924. It was on display at Basingstoke in mid 2001. Ten years previously, the HCMS exhibited no fewer than seven of its charges at the big steam fair in Dorset.

Tasker of Andover, Hampshire, made wagons between 1910 and 1925, producing only around 120 in that time. The majority were of the 5 ton type but some 3 and 6 tonners and one 10 ton wagon were also made. Just one example of the make survives – and is to be found in a Basingstoke museum. In the same museum is another sole survivor from the same county – that from the Basingstoke firm of Wallis & Steevens. This firm made almost 130 wagons between 1906 and 1924; most were 5 ton and the remainder were 3 tonners.

Although this wagon looks remarkably like a Foden, it is an example of a Danks, made at Oldbury in the West Midlands. It was owned by a Leeds-based firm of haulage contractors, who obtained it from J. Riley & Sons of Hapton, Burnley, Lancashire. It was Danks No. 106 of 1916 and was scrapped around a decade and a half later. (Photograph: L&DTEC collection)

Undertype wagons

Many of the early wagons were primitive, with a boiler at the front with the driver and an engine mounted beneath the chassis, the drive to the rear axle being either by chain or by gears. Some firms stayed with their own choice of design, believing that it was the best; others ventured into both forms. Although undertype wagons were mainly fitted with vertical boilers, both Mann's and Thornycroft made some with a short locomotive-type horizontal boiler as well.

Garrett built its first wagon, an undertype, in 1904, followed by one in 1906 and another in 1908. However, many of its products were overtypes – a good example of a firm producing relatively large quantities of both and, by so doing, being able to supply whichever type the customer wanted. Garrett's total, including the early versions, was some 310 undertype wagons – in ranges from 4 to 8 tons on four wheels and up to 10/15 tonners on six wheels – between 1921 and 1931.

Leyland – known as the Lancashire Steam Motor Company until 1907 – took over Coulthard and produced solely undertypes, the first of which was a chain-drive 4 ton model that competed in the first Liverpool Trial in

Below: Garrett QL type wagon No. 34841 of 1926, pictured at Israel Newton's Boilerworks in Idle, Bradford, during a visit by members of the Road Locomotive Society in October 2000.

Below: Garrett six-wheel undertype wagon No. 35355 (KR 1628) was new in January 1930 to haulage contractor Albert Chapman of Ashford in Kent. This variation of the QL model had an asymmetrical cab so that the driver sat adjacent to the boiler on its right, and that corner of the cab was square – giving a much enhanced view of the road ahead – but the left-hand side was curved in what had become the conventional manner for this type of vehicle.

Above: *Leyland wagon No. F2/28-1682 (TB 1336) was made in the place of the same name in Lancashire. It was in use from 1920 until 1935 by sugar refiners Fairrie & Co Ltd in Liverpool and was No. 7 in that firm's fleet. With its trailer, it could carry around 10 tons of sugar. (Photograph: courtesy of J. N. E. Fairrie)*

1898. The firm very quickly moved on to a 5 ton and then a 6 ton version and by 1908 had developed its 'K' type vehicle, which was shaft drive. Leyland made petrol wagons in parallel with steam-powered ones and eventually, in 1911, developed its 'F' class, which lasted until the end of production of steam vehicles in 1926. This latter was a 6 tonner with chain drive, eventually being updated from a water tube boiler to a thimble tube variety; this final type was designated 'F2'.

Mann's of Leeds produced undertypes in around 1904 – to comply with the Heavy Motor Car Act – but was more notable for its production of overtype wagons, carts and tractors. However, after the First World War, in common with other makers, the firm set about a re-design and came up with the 'Express' wagon – a very similar looking vehicle to the Sentinel of the time. Indeed, Mann's used a derivation of Sentinel's boiler in this wagon, which was launched in 1924. Competition arose from other Leeds builders such as Fowler,

Left: Yorkshire 'WG' type wagon No. 2108 of 1927 languished in a shed in Castleford, West Yorkshire, for many years and was restored by Walter Fearnley, one of the well-known family who did so much to promote steam events in West Yorkshire in the early rallying years. It was subsequently owned by Tom Varley and in 2002 was in the West Country.

Right: A major restoration was required by the late Tom Varley on this 3 ton 1917 Yorkshire wagon No. 940, which he rescued in an extremely poor condition from a Leeds scrapyard in the late 1960s. At Harewood Rally, West Yorkshire, in 1970, it is well appreciated by an admiring crowd.

Yorkshire No. 656 (registration number U 2831) was one of four similar tanker wagons supplied to the Anglo-Mexican Petroleum Products Co Ltd for the transport of its commodities. A tanker-trailer enabled a greater quantity of liquid to be carried at one time. The wagon was built in 1914 and it seems strange in the light of modern safety requirements that steam wagons should have been used for the haulage of this type of product. A steam-driven pump is fitted at the rear of both the wagon and its trailer. (Photograph: L&DTEC collection)

which was just entering into the steam wagon market, and the next-door firm of Yorkshire, located, like Mann's, in Pepper Road. Although the 'Express' design had much to commend it, it was possibly outclassed by others and only around a dozen were produced before the firm folded in 1928. Unfortunately none remains today.

The very well-known 'Sentinel' brand of wagon was started by marine engineers Alley & McLellan of Polmadie, Glasgow. It bought the patent rights of the Simson & Bibby wagon of 1903, seeing in this the potential of the steam wagon market. The first Sentinel design of 1905 had much to commend it and, while many of the other early makers quickly fell by the wayside, this type, with various

Left: What better sponsor could one have for a steam lorry than a coal-based fuel consultant? Sentinel Standard model No. 3899 of 1921 was sold to Sweden some time after its appearance at the 1988 show in Dorset and went on display at an automobile museum there. It subsequently returned to the United Kingdom and will again be displayed at steam events.

Right: One of the former Brown Bayley Steels of Sheffield fleet of Sentinel Standard wagons, which remains in that firm's livery, is No. 1286 of 1916. It can be seen in the Glasgow Museum of Transport. The Sentinel Company originated as the Glasgow firm of Alley & McLellan in Polmadie and its early products were built at that location before the firm moved to Shrewsbury – hence this wagon being on display in Glasgow.

21

Above: *The author's introduction to steam wagons was at Fearnley's yard by the river in Castleford, West Yorkshire. The family was exhibiting them in the late 1950s and one of the earliest on the rally circuit was 'Ronnie's wagon' – Sentinel No. 1465 of 1916. It was built then as a 'Standard' type and was usually described in rally programmes as such, but it was so heavily rebuilt by the makers for their own use during the Second World War, along with others, that its later basis was really that of a 'Super' model. On the right is 'Uncle Walter' Fearnley's Foden wagon, No. 13120, dating from 1928.*

Below: *Sentinel Super wagon No. 7591, which was new in 1928, resting on the weighbridge at the National Railway Museum, York. The occasion was a Road and Rail event, depicting some of the vehicles from a bygone age that could have worked in and around railway stations and goods yards. A weight ticket was issued to the owner before he moved off.*

Above: *Tom Varley was a prolific restorer of steam wagons and he brought several back to Britain from Australia that would have been unlikely to have been rebuilt for many years, if ever, had they remained there. The British rally scene would have been all the poorer had Tom not done this – and he unfortunately died before his great achievements in this field could be fully recognised. One such example was this unique Atkinson No. 72 of 1918, which he brought back in 1976 and restored. It then received a paint scheme appropriate to its commercial operating days.*

improvements, continued in production as the Sentinel 'Standard' wagon until 1922. A total of around 3,750 were made, making it the most numerous type of steam wagon ever. In the meantime, in order to provide room for expansion, the firm moved to Shrewsbury in 1915, becoming The Sentinel Waggon Works until 1920, when, after incorporation, a further name change took place. It later became the Sentinel Waggon Works (1936) Ltd as a fully owned subsidiary of Metal Industries Ltd.

It should be pointed out that, from the outset, this firm's registered name and its spelling of 'wagon' in literature and on its builder's plates was with two 'g's – 'waggon' – but to maintain consistency within this book all text references to wagons are spelt with one 'g'.

As an improvement to the Standard, the firm brought out the Super version in 1923, laying out the factory on the flow-line principle in order to produce the wagons quickly, and around 1,550 of these were

Above left: *A worthy prizewinner: 'HMS Sultan', 1930 Sentinel Super wagon No. 8393, ventured as far north as York in 1990 to receive a Steam Heritage Award in the scheme sponsored at that time by British Coal – and, at the same time, engaged in some advance publicity for the Great Railway Show, which had just opened at the National Railway Museum where the award ceremony was held. The wagon is normally resident in Gosport, Hampshire, and is cared for by volunteers from staff at the naval establishment after which it is named, and which has owned it since 1960.*

Above right: *Sentinel Super wagon No. 8381 at an event near York in the early 1990s. This was part of a large collection of engines formerly owned by Tom Paisley of Holywell, St Ives, Cambridgeshire, who died in 1980. A 'Sale of the Decade' took place after his death but this wagon did not feature in it as it was retained by the family. (Photograph: R. A. Daniel)*

Left: *Auctions can be sad occasions and this one was particularly poignant for it came about after the owner of this Sentinel DG4 wagon was killed during a disagreement with a customer of his garage. Always an innovator, Ted Ashton from Brotherton, North Yorkshire, had experimented with several different methods of firing the wagon, No. 8694 of 1932, and had even used gas as a fuel in an attempt to improve its performance. The auctioneer's signwriter has made the usual mistake in the spelling of the wagon maker's name by including a letter 'a' in it.*

Right: *An unusual Sentinel is this SDDG4 model (Shaft Drive Double Gear 4-wheel) of 1930, No. 8448. It was a prototype and marked the transition between the then regular chain-drive wagons and the later 'S' models – with their S (shaft) drive arrangement – which were introduced in 1933.*

made in batches. This new design dispelled the myth that vertical boilers were poor steamers; so much so that Foden, a traditional overtype wagon maker, and others such as Atkinson, Garrett, Clayton, Leyland and Mann's, all brought out new models that looked very similar to the Sentinel. For Sentinel this was a turnabout, for it was only in around 1911–12 that the firm marketed an overtype wagon in an attempt to compete with Foden's, whose products then were becoming very popular.

After the success of the Super model, it was the turn of the DG – or Double Geared wagon – which was made from 1927 in four-, six- and eight-wheeled versions. A design of floating bogie was produced

With its ashpan down and driver David Parkin with poker in hand, Sentinel S4 wagon No. 8942 of January 1934 is having its fire attended to. The access is from the side as the wagon's front axle is in the way of a straightforward front dropping arrangement as seen on earlier models.

for the larger types – the DG6 and DG8. Only eight of the latter were made, all tippers. The total production run was around 850.

In 1933, what can perhaps be described as the ultimate in steam wagon design – the Sentinel 'S' model – came on the market. This again was produced as four-, six- and also the massive eight-wheeled versions. Many automatic features were available, including water replenishment and stoking, as required. Some four hundred of these were made before the Second World War – and around a hundred after the war. The total Sentinel production of steam wagons and tractors was about 6,500. Somewhat surprisingly, this was around the same number built by Foden, Sentinel's main competitor. Remarkably, over

Sentinel timber tractor No. 9097 was new in 1934 and is pictured in 1971 at the railway depot at Tyseley, Birmingham, on the occasion of a steam gathering there (upper picture). At its rear is mounted a separate engine for winching purposes (lower picture). This is a DG type machine, produced at a time when the main output of the Shrewsbury works was concerned with shaft drive 'S' model wagons. (Photographs: D. P. Haynes)

24

A superbly posed shot of a 'modern' shaft-drive Sentinel wagon – an S4 model – built in 1934, taken outside the Shrewsbury works. No. 8970 originally went to a Sheffield brewery and is now in preservation in South Yorkshire.

150 Sentinels have survived in preservation around the world.

One firm late in production of its steam wagon was John Fowler of Leeds. This firm was well known for many other types of road steam vehicle but it was not until 1924, when others were giving up, that John Fowler decided it was time to enter this market. Because of its long association with local authorities involved in the steam rolling trade, the majority of the firm's wagons found use with such organisations – for haulage, road cleansing and gulley emptying – while others were used by road-making firms and were fitted with tar-spraying equipment. Several were exported, some going to Bogota in Colombia and others to South Africa. The firm's last wagon, a gulley emptier, was sold to Warsaw, Poland, in 1934. Just one representative from this maker still survives – a Tom Varley restoration.

Right: On completion of restoration by its owners in 1968, Sentinel S4 wagon No. 9075 of 1934 was given the name 'Holmevalian' after the location, Holmfirth, West Yorkshire, where the joint owners lived. It is a name that the wagon retains to the present day.

Left: Sentinel S4 No. 9003, dating from 1934, was one of the first in the long line of steam vehicles owned and restored by the late Tom Varley and named after the Pendle district in north Lancashire where he lived. This is 'Pendle Lady' at Harewood, West Yorkshire, in 1968.

The commercial demise – and subsequent rebirth – of steam wagons

The halcyon days for steam wagon makers were probably those leading up to the First World War. However, a far greater number of manufacturers was active earlier in the 1900s and many in Great Britain had disappeared by around 1910, when the boom years for the smaller makers ended. Most of the others had gone by the end of the 1920s, their demise being hastened by the large numbers of petrol-engined wagons that became available and were sold off as surplus after the end of the war. Competition was accelerated in the late 1920s and early 1930s with the advent of the diesel engine and many petrol-engined lorries were converted to diesel in order to make them more cost-effective.

Notwithstanding this situation, it was government legislation relating to major changes in taxation and vehicle weights that put the majority of solid-rubber tyred vehicles off the road in the early 1930s. Many felt that these were anti-steam measures and they certainly resulted in large numbers of the older types of steam wagon being scrapped. Between 1931 and 1936 some five thousand steam wagons disappeared from the roads. Some newer ones were re-wheeled – mainly by Sentinel – but many hauliers immediately turned to oil-engined vehicles (which did not have weighty boilers) in order to remain competitive.

Competition in the steam wagon market had waned by this time. With this legislation – and the competition from the newly introduced diesel engines – steam for road transport purposes was on its way out.

Owned by a North Yorkshire enthusiast, this 1918 Sentinel Standard wagon resides in Norfolk. In 2000 it was painted for promotional purposes in the livery of a local brewery for which it has delivered beer, and it also attended the Norwich Beer Festival. At one time it worked in the Brown Bayley steelworks in Sheffield and was in service there until the mid 1960s. No. 1960 is pictured at Weeting Rally, Norfolk, in 2001.

Left: *A fine example of a Sentinel DG6 solid-tyred wagon pictured outside the works at Shrewsbury. It was No. 8335 and was supplied to a Yorkshire customer at the end of July 1930. The houses in the background were built by the firm for its employees and this location was a favourite for official photographs. This wagon was returned by the Yorkshire Dyeware & Chemical Co to Sentinel in 1932 and converted to a DG4 on pneumatic tyres (see page 30).*

Sentinel alone continued in this field until after the Second World War. Foden, however, produced its Speed-6 and Speed-12 undertype models in 1930 – but they were not particularly successful and, although several were sold, they lasted in production only until 1932.

Sentinel developed an answer to this vexed question with the introduction of its 'S' (shaft-drive) model on pneumatic tyres in 1933 and for a time these were very popular – being made in some quantity up to 1937.

A successful American steam car engineer, Abner Doble, came to work for the Shrewsbury firm in 1931 and continued the development of the steam wagon with an oil-fired flash-steam boiler that generated pressures up to 1,500 pounds per square inch. His ideas quickly reached the prototype stage and were successfully trialled but he left in 1936 as a result of the company's financial difficulties, for which he was partly to blame. No more development work took place as the war intervened and the two experimental lorries that had been built were scrapped soon after the war ended. Abner Doble later continued his efforts elsewhere, while Warren Doble, his brother, had developed similar ideas on contract to Henschel in Germany up to around 1936.

Steam wagons were found to be an ideal vehicle for road maintenance firms because their boilers served as ready-made heating equipment. Many were thus converted into tar-sprayers and other

A real workhorse at many early rallies was Sentinel S4 No. 8992, 'Prince'. Seen with both cab doors open, it was originally a flat-bed wagon and saw commercial use in Lancashire. In preservation days, in the ownership of the late Ernie Liversedge from Doncaster, South Yorkshire, it was fitted with a large three-section tank, together with a small steam engine from a Locomobile steam car to drive a pump, and was used to ferry water to engines at events. After passing to other owners, this 1934 wagon was sold to Sydney, Australia, in 1986. (Photograph: D. P. Haynes)

In the latter days of steam wagons, many were converted into tar-sprayers – since they were able to keep the tar tanks warm with a steam heating coil fed from the boiler. This Yorkshire 'WG' class of wagon was originally supplied to the Bradford Corporation in 1932 and ended its days with David Wood & Co of Yeadon near Leeds, contractors to the North Riding County Council and others. The wagon, No. 2189, is pictured at Stockton-on-the-Forest near York in July 1952. (Photograph: P. N. Williams)

types of road-making vehicle. W. & J. Glossop of Hipperholme, West Yorkshire, was probably the largest operator of this type of vehicle, owning more than 130 over the years, some of which lasted until the late 1950s.

Those steam wagons available for haulage during the Second World War continued in service, some of them right through until the early 1950s. The Suez oil crisis in 1956 brought several steam vehicles out of retirement – including one Sentinel wagon that worked on contract to a brewery in Kent delivering beer, and they were also to be seen on Liverpool docks until 1961. Another fuel crisis in September 2000 caused by the blockading of refineries saw one steam wagon delivering

Sentinel tar-sprayer No. 8666 of 1932 (which incorrectly carries plate 6400) was previously with Yorkshire tar-spraying contractor W. J. Glossop, who restored it to working order after its commercial days were finished. It is pictured (above) at the Barleylands Steam Rally in Essex in 1999 during a demonstration of road-making. (Right) Tar is being sprayed on to the stone foundations for the roadway, which have been consolidated and rolled by a steam roller. Small chippings are being spread by hand on top of the tar and these will be rolled by the following steam roller – out of the picture on the right – to compress them into the tar and make them stick on top of the prepared surface. Members of the public are kept at a safe distance.

Left: *Just after the Second World War, wagons for bulk transport were at a premium – as was the supply of oil-based fuels. An enterprising firm in Leeds, the Central Haulage & Motor Company, run by Len and Wilf Cole, who had operated steam wagons over a long period, obtained a couple of redundant ones from Shropshire County Council, one of which it used to provide spares for the other. This was pressed into service in the early 1950s to move coal from Methley Park opencast site, close to Leeds, to the nearby power station. This is a six-wheel S-type tipping model and was built in 1934, No. 9043.*

Below: *Still at work in the 1950s in the docks area of Liverpool is this Sentinel Super wagon No. 6258. Originally purchased by J. A. Webster & Co Ltd of Trafford Park, Manchester, in 1925, it passed to William Harper & Sons, Liverpool, in 1948. The photograph, by John Meredith, was taken on a poor November day in 1951. Although many of the wagons in use around Liverpool at this time have survived into the preservation era, this particular vehicle unfortunately has not.*

beer in Norfolk, although this was more of a publicity exercise than a commercial requirement.

The construction of steam wagons in England had, to all intents and purposes, finished by the start of the war. There was one brief excursion into the realms of fantasy after that, however, when Sentinel at Shrewsbury received an order from the Argentinian government in 1949 for a batch of one hundred wagons to carry coal from the inland Rio Turbio coal mines in Tierra del Fuego some 150 miles (240 km) to a freezer plant on the coast. The steam wagons were intended to be only a stopgap as a railway was ultimately planned for this purpose. How many of the hundred actually reached their destination has never been fully

Several steam wagons remained in service until the late 1960s in Sheffield. Working for Brown Bayley Steels, they were used to carry heavy hot ingots of steel around the works during the production process. Although there were always many hot shards of steel on the ground, the wagons' solid tyres did not puncture and they were thus ideal for the job. They were disposed of in the early 1970s. This is No. 1716, fleet No. 9, and with the steelworks from new in 1917. The wagon was still working in 1968, when this picture was taken, but was retired very soon afterwards and is now in Essex.

Right: *The same wagon as seen at the top of page 27 after conversion by Sentinel in 1932. Legislation introduced around that time discriminated against heavy solid-tyred vehicles by taxing them considerably more than pneumatic-tyred ones and many such vehicles were withdrawn and scrapped. This example, however, continued in service, having been put on to pneumatics by the maker, and was later bought by Walter B. Bradwell of Rastrick, West Yorkshire, who in turn sold it to Briar Silk Transport Co of Brierfield, Lancashire, in 1942.*

Sentinel made trailers in order to increase the wagon's load-carrying capability. This pneumatic-tyred trailer, No. 8731, was supplied to Yorkshire Dyeware in August 1932 for use with its newly converted DG4 wagon, illustrated above. The firm produced almost 550 trailers in total.

established but some wagons performed the required task for a number of years in very difficult circumstances until the completion of the railway in 1955. At least one of these wagons survives in poor condition at Rio Galegos and another is in semi-derelict state at the Zoo Luján in Buenos Aires province, Argentina.

After the Argentinian order, a six-wheel dumper truck was made in 1951 for experimental purposes – the National Coal Board used it successfully for a while but felt disinclined to order a large number and it was then sold to a quarry at Penderyn, near Brecon in Powys, where it saw considerable use. It was eventually fitted with a diesel engine because of the low temperatures experienced, which caused its water pipes to freeze. This same problem and solution also caused the demise of the final Sentinel wagon, which was constructed in 1952 by Sentinel's northern agent, Thomas Hill of Whiston, South Yorkshire. It was a four-wheel dump truck that was built out of spares and sold to a Derbyshire quarry for stone haulage.

By this time, traction engine rallies had started and at one of the first, at Appleford, Oxfordshire, in the early 1950s, one enthusiast journeyed to the event from Shropshire in his Sentinel. Because it was not a traction engine, it was left in the car park for the duration of the event but, as time progressed, steam wagons became accepted into the fold and now regularly attend similar rallies, which are held

Robey overtype wagon No. 42522 of 1926 – one of only two survivors of its type in the United Kingdom – as rebuilt by Rundles of New Bolingbroke, Lincolnshire. The advent of the rally movement has seen considerable interest in rare examples of different marques. (Photograph: Alan Rundle)

Right: *A 1990s-built steam wagon called 'Typhoo'. It was created by a clever South Yorkshire engineer, using a Sentinel railway locomotive boiler and vertical engine (similar to some steam wagon engines, only larger) mounted on an ERF six-wheeled wagon chassis. As a development exercise it was a very interesting project. It is pictured in 1994, when it became mobile, and has subsequently been completed, with panelling fully enclosing the vehicle, which has a fine turn of speed. The owner has never disguised the fact that it is a 'new' vehicle and of his own making – and it draws crowds of curious onlookers whenever it is displayed.*

periodically all over Britain and also in many other countries. Mostly privately owned, they are now an essential adjunct to the rest of this expanding leisure movement.

Many of the drivers employed by haulage contractors in the inter-war years used to boast about their own favourites and argue about which maker's steam wagon was the best. Perhaps the numbers of surviving wagons in the United Kingdom provide the best evidence on which to make this judgement. There are no representatives from Burrell or Allchin and only one or two from such makers as Wallis & Steevens, Ransomes, Mann's, Foster, Tasker and Thornycroft. There are a few from Garrett, Clayton & Shuttleworth and Yorkshire, but there are plenty of Fodens (eighty-three) and even more Sentinels (ninety-nine). Not surprisingly, the arguments as to which is, or was, the best steam wagon continue on the rally fields of today.

On two occasions – in 1976 and 1999 – several steam wagons made the long journey of almost a thousand miles from John O'Groats to Land's End. The 1999 'marathon' involved some ten Sentinels, which successfully completed the run, proving that well maintained steam wagons are still capable of doing this many decades after they were built. This is tribute indeed to the skills of the British engineers and craftsmen who designed and constructed them all those years ago.

Foreign-built wagons

Developments on the continent of Europe virtually paralleled those in England in the early twentieth century; a number of established railway locomotive manufacturers who had the appropriate equipment produced steam wagons and other smaller firms also attempted to break into the burgeoning market.

French manufacturers included Purrey of Bordeaux (later Exshaw), whose wagons were demonstrated in Britain in 1913. In addition, De Dion Bouton in 1899, Scotte, Serpollet and Turgan-Foy also produced either steam brakes or wagons. In Holland, W. A. Holk designed a wagon for the firm of J. & A. van der Schnijtt in 1907.

The Berlin-based firm of L. Schwartzkopff (later Berliner Maschinenbau AG) pictured a Thornycroft-type steam wagon in its seventy-fifth anniversary book produced in 1929, which was indicated as being contemporary with the firm's steam rollers (1881) and steam tramway locomotives (1882). This wagon was of a type that Schwartzkopff built under licence from the British firm. However, Thornycroft's records indicate that it did supply an early wagon (works No. 50) to BMAG in November 1900 – from which one may deduce that the details in the German firm's book are incorrect.

Another German manufacturer was Hannoversche Maschinenbau Aktien Gesellschaft (later HANOMAG). This firm used the Stoltz-type high pressure boiler as the steam provider in its 1909-built wagons. This system was also used in wagons, under licence, by Friedrich Krupp in Kiel and Eisenwerke Gaggenau in Gaggenau. The Swiss firm Schweizerische Lokomotiv- und Maschinenfabrik (SLM)

Purrey (later Exshaw) was one of only a handful of steam wagon builders in France. The works was at Bordeaux and this example, built in 1906, has a two-compartment tipping body arrangement on the rear. The steam generator was a water-tube type, mounted behind the driver, and the engine was beneath the floor.
(Photograph: Berliet Fondation, Lyon)

Left: *Sentinel Super tractor of 1928, No. 7527, at Dordrecht, Holland, at the 'Dordt in Stoom' event in 2000. The machine has been in Holland since 1988 and has been roaded (driven under its own power) quite extensively in preservation to other countries in Europe as well.*

Below: *A Foden with a box van body at 'Dordt in Stoom', Holland. No. 13624 of 1930 was a former West Riding of Yorkshire County Council machine which went to Ellis of Harrogate for scrap in 1939. Later resurrected, and after considerable restoration, it has become a familiar part of the southern rally scene. In 1996, the wagon was driven from the Dutch ferry terminal to Dordrecht by the late Mick Tuxworth, pictured attending to the wagon, and was later used for television and product promotional purposes in the Netherlands.*

Above: *Yorkshire No. 2049 dates from July 1924 and is seen just inside its shed on the outskirts of Melbourne, Australia. This 7 ton 'WF' wagon, now named 'Ethel' and fitted with a bus-type body, has been restored over a considerable number of years by Dave Mickle and friends.*

On the right is 1928 Robey six-wheeled articulated wagon No. 43757 in Sri Lanka in early 2002. It is the only articulated steam wagon known to exist in the world and was previously used to transport goods in the Colombo docks area for the British Ceylon Corporation. This unique survivor and the adjacent four-wheeled Robey wagon No. 42888 of 1925 remained in service until the early 1980s, when they were withdrawn and put into store. (Photograph: P. A. Warby)

Although steam wagon makers in Europe were not very plentiful, the Schweizerische Lokomotiv- und Maschinenfabrik (SLM) at Winterthur, Switzerland, entered the market in 1898 at the same time as such early vehicles were being built in England. The SLM examples seemed to be more substantial than their contemporary British counterparts and, surprisingly, only a few examples were made. SLM later adopted, under licence, the high pressure (50 atm) German system of Peter Stolz of Berlin. Better known for the many railway locomotives of all gauges that it constructed, SLM also built some steam rollers in 1923. The Stolz-type wagon pictured was built for the town of Winterthur in 1909 and was fitted with a tank, presumably for street-watering purposes. (Photograph courtesy of Ernst Huwyler and the Archive of Dampfwalzen Club Schweiz)

at Winterthur also made a few wagons in the English style from around 1898 but this design was not perpetuated and the firm also later marketed Stolz-type wagons, as did the Société Anonyme des Générateurs Economiques (SAGE) in Paris.

In the mid 1920s, Sentinel of Shrewsbury made an arrangement with Skoda in Plzen, Czechoslovakia, and some fifty Super-Sentinels were exported to the firm. Around 160 wagons and tractors were also built there under licence to the same design – as Skoda-Sentinels. At least three of these are still in existence. Garrett had a similar arrangement with the Adamov Engineering Works in the same country – but how many, if any, of this firm's wagons were actually produced there is not known.

In the early 1930s, while Abner Doble's experiments at Sentinel were still in progress, his brother Warren moved on to work with Henschel in Germany and continued to develop similar ideas in the field of high pressure and high efficiency steam road wagons. A number of such lorries and some rail vehicles were built for the Deutsche Reichbahn (German Railways) before the Second World War but it is understood that papers relating to these have all been lost and unfortunately none of these

A Skoda-Sentinel plate, as fitted to steam wagons built in Czechoslovakia in the 1920s.

In the early 1900s, the Buffalo Steam Roller Co of Springfield, Ohio, along with other makers of such machinery in the United States, decided to enter the steam wagon market since the essential equipment was already in place for manufacturing the bulk of the vehicle. Not many were produced, however, but this end-tipping version exhibits a distinctly English look at the front. The maker's plate on the side panel in front of the flywheel seems to be identical to that used on the company's steam rollers. (Photograph: Ray Drake collection)

potentially interesting Henschel steam vehicles seems to have survived the war.

It was perhaps inevitable also that in the United States of America a proliferation of small firms made relatively small numbers of vehicles. In addition some of the better established traction engine makers also produced their own versions of steam wagons.

Maurice Kelly's American book (see 'Further reading') says that some wagons made by Buffalo-Springfield worked in Britain. He writes:

> According to a driver who worked in London during the 1920s, Mr Harry Crudgington, there were five of these engines working for Messrs Charrington, the well known Mile End brewers, and they were imported from the United States in 1920. He also told the writer that some of this batch had been made by the White Corporation of Cleveland, Ohio.

These wagons were thought to have been made from about 1917 to 1922.

Very many steam wagons were driven through the gateway below. This is the Sentinel Works in Shrewsbury, watched over by the firm's trademark – a 'Sentinel' in full-plate armour. This same trademark, with the accompanying motto 'Ever watchful & on the alert', was also to be seen on Sentinel's works plates (see also page 34). Latterly the site was owned by Perkins, the diesel engine manufacturer, but following another change in ownership it has now become somewhat neglected.

The *World's Commercial Vehicles 1830–1964* records almost 160 steam wagon makers. Of these, thirty-one were based in the United States, thirty-five in Europe and no fewer than ninety-two in Britain, including six in Scotland. In addition there were around twenty makers that built only steam public service vehicles, located in similar proportions to the previously noted categories. There were also some twenty manufacturers of steam-powered light vans, of which the majority were based in the USA.

Miscellaneous versions of 'steam wagons' also existed, such as self-propelled fire engines, street sweepers, haulage tractors, buses and agricultural tractors. However, the most interesting from a technical point of view may have been the 'Turbine' steam wagon made in the United States in 1904. It was propelled by a steam turbine driving a generator, with ultimately an electric motor drive to the wheels.

During the Second World War and just afterwards, there was a surge of interest in steam wagons in various parts of Europe and they were produced by several manufacturers, or converted from petrol-engined ones, since oil supplies were at a premium or non-existent. Makers that produced such wagons during this time were Dias (1946), Lenz & Butenuth (1948), Lowa (1946–50) and Sachsenberg (1943–44) – all in Germany – and Yugo-Slovenska (1948) in Yugoslavia.

Steam wagon manufacturers

Some notable British makers

William Allchin & Company Limited, Northampton.

Alley & McLellan Limited (later Sentinel), Glasgow.

Atkinson & Company Limited (later Atkinson-Walker Wagons Limited), Preston, Lancashire.

Aveling & Porter Limited, Rochester, Kent.

Charles Burrell & Sons Limited, Thetford, Norfolk.

Clarkson Limited, Chelmsford, Essex.

Clayton & Shuttleworth Limited (later Clayton Wagons Limited), Lincoln.

Edwin Foden, Sons & Company Limited, Sandbach, Cheshire.

William Foster & Company Limited, Lincoln.

John Fowler & Company Limited, Leeds, West Yorkshire.

Richard Garrett & Sons Limited, Leiston, Suffolk.

Leyland Motors Limited (previously The Lancashire Steam Motor Company), Leyland, Lancashire.

Mann & Charlesworth Limited (later Mann's Patent Steam Cart & Wagon Company Limited), Leeds, West Yorkshire.

Ransomes, Sims & Jefferies Limited, Ipswich, Suffolk.

Robey & Company Limited, Lincoln.

The Sentinel Waggon Works Limited (previously Alley & McLellan), Shrewsbury, Shropshire.

William Tasker & Sons Limited, Andover, Hampshire.

The Thornycroft Steam Wagon Company Limited, Chiswick, London (later Basingstoke, Hampshire).

Wallis & Steevens Limited, Basingstoke, Hampshire.

The Yorkshire Patent Steam Wagon Company Limited, Leeds, West Yorkshire (previously Yorkshire Steam Motor Company, also The Yorkshire Commercial Motor Company).

There are also over sixty other recorded manufacturers of steam wagons in the United Kingdom.

Some foreign makers

American Coulthard, Boston, Massachusetts, USA.

American Steam Truck Company, Lansing, Michigan, USA (1912–13).

American Steam Truck Company, Elgin, Illinois, USA (1918–22).

Aultman Company, Canton, Ohio, USA.

Baker Motors Incorporated, Cleveland, Ohio, USA.

Baldwin Motor Wagon Company, Providence, Rhode Island, USA.

Bell & Waring Steam Vehicle Company, New York, USA.

Buffalo Steam Roller Company, Springfield, Ohio, USA.

Chaboche, Paris, France.

Edward S. Clark Steam Automobiles, Dorchester, Massachusetts, USA.

Corwin Manufacturing Company, Peabody, Massachusetts, USA.

Cunningham Engineering Company, Boston, Massachusetts, USA.

De Dion Bouton, Paris, France.

Doble Steam Motors Corporation, Emeryville, California, USA.

Gardner-Serpollet (later Darracq-Serpollet), Paris, France.

Grout Bros Automobile Company, Orange, Massachusetts, USA.

J. T. Halsey Motor Truck Company, Philadelphia, Pennsylvania, USA.

Hannoversche Maschinenbau AG (later HANOMAG), Hannover, Germany.

Henschel und Sohne, Kassel, Germany.

Herschmann, Brooklyn, New York, USA.

Janney-Steinmetz & Company, Philadelphia, Pennsylvania, USA.

Johnson Service Company, Milwaukee, Wisconsin, USA.

O. S. Kelly, Springfield, Ohio, USA.

Massachusetts Steam Wagon Company, Boston, Massachusetts, USA.

Michigan Steam Motor Company, Detroit, Michigan, USA.

Milwaukee Automobile Company, Milwaukee, Wisconsin, USA.

Mobile Company of America, New York, USA.

Morgan Motor Company, Worcester, Massachusetts, USA.

V. Purrey (later Purrey-Exshaw), Bordeaux, France.

Schwartzkopff, Berlin, Germany.

Schweizerische Lokomotiv- und Maschinenfabrik, Winterthur, Switzerland.

Stanley Steam Motor Corporation, Chicago, Illinois, USA.

Steam Automotive Works (later Steam-O-Truck), Denver, Colorado, USA.

Steamotor Truck Company (later Amalgamated Machinery Corporation), Chicago, Illinois, USA.

Stoltz, Berlin, Germany.

Turgan-Foy, Levallois-Perret, France.

J. & A. van der Schnijtt, The Netherlands.

White Motor Company, Cleveland, Ohio, USA.

Winslow Boiler & Engineering Company, Chicago, Illinois, USA.

Zappa & Schars, Bordeaux, France.

Further reading

Chanuc, Lucien. *Ces Étonnants Véhicules à Vapeur.* Editions de l'Ormet, France, 1995.

Clark, Ronald H. *The Development of the English Steam Wagon.* Goose & Son, 1963.

Georgano, G. N. *The World's Commercial Vehicles 1830–1964.* Temple Press Books, 1965.

Hughes, W. J., and Thomas, Joseph L. *The Sentinel: Volume I, 1875–1930.* David & Charles, 1973.

Kelly, Maurice A. *The Overtype Steam Road Wagon.* Goose & Son, 1971.

Kelly, Maurice A. *The Undertype Steam Road Wagon.* Goose & Son, 1975.

Kelly, Maurice A. *The American Steam Traction Engine.* CMS Publishing, 1995.

Lane, Michael R. *The Story of the Steam Plough Works: John Fowler & Sons Ltd.* Northgate Publishing Company, 1980.

Lane, Michael R. *The Story of the Wellington Foundry: A History of William Foster.* Unicorn Press, 1997.

Lane, Michael R. *The Story of the St Nicholas Works: A History of Charles Burrell.* AGM Projects, 1999.

Norris, William. *Modern Steam Road Wagons.* Longman Green & Company, 1906; reprinted by David & Charles, 1972.

Thomas, Anthony R. and Joseph L. *The Sentinel: Volume II, 1930–1980.* Woodpecker Publications, 1987.

True, J. B. *Traction Engine Register.* Southern Counties Historic Vehicle Preservation Trust, April 2000.

Whitehead, Robert. *Wallis & Steevens: A History.* Road Locomotive Society, 1983.

Whitehead, R. A. *Kaleidoscope of Steam Wagons.* Marshall, Harris & Baldwin, 1979.

Whitehead, R. A. *Garrett Wagons, part 1,* 1994; *Garrett Wagons, part 2,* 1995. Whitehead & Partners. A series on the make of Garrett.

1916 Mann's 5 ton steam wagon No. 1120 was restored many years ago in Kent but was sold in 2000 to the Hampshire area. It carries a 'lift van' body, which was popular with house removal contractors since it could be removed and left behind at one location for loading before being picked up and transported to the people's new home, where again it could be left for unloading – without tying up the wagon for all of the time. In this respect, it was part of an early form of containerisation. (Photograph: Peter Kelly)

Places to visit

Bass Museum, Horninglow Street, Burton upon Trent, Staffordshire DE14 1YQ. Telephone: 01283 511000 or 0845 6000 598. Website: www.bass-museum.com/main.htm

Beamish: The North of England Open Air Museum, Beamish, County Durham DH9 0RG. Telephone: 0191 370 4000. Website: www.beamish.org.uk

Bressingham Steam Museum Trust, Thetford Road, Bressingham, Diss, Norfolk IP22 2AB. Telephone: 01379 686900. Website: www.bressingham.co.uk

British Commercial Vehicle Museum, King Street, Leyland, Lancashire PR5 1LE. Telephone: 01772 451011.

Glasgow Museum of Transport, Kelvin Hall, 1 Bunhouse Road, Glasgow G3 8PD. Telephone: 0141 221 9600.

Grampian Transport Museum, Alford, Aberdeen AB33 8AE. Telephone: 01975 562292. Website: www.gtm.org.uk

Levens Hall, Kendal, Cumbria LA8 0PD. Telephone: 01539 560321. Website: www.levenshall.co.uk

Milestones – Hampshire's Living History Museum, West Ham Leisure Park, Churchill Way West, Basingstoke, Hampshire RG12 6YR. Telephone: 01256 477766. Website www.milestones-museum.com

Strumpshaw Hall Steam Museum, Strumpshaw, Norwich NR13 4HR. Telephone: 01603 714535.

Summerlee Heritage Park, Heritage Way, Coatbridge, Lanarkshire ML5 1QD. Telephone: 01236 431261. Website: www.northlan.gov.uk

Thinktank at millenniumpoint, Curzon Street, Digbeth, Birmingham B4 7XG. Telephone: 0121 202 2222. Website: www.thinktank.ac

The Thursford Collection, Thursford Green, Thursford, Fakenham, Norfolk NR21 0AS. Telephone: 01328 878477.

In 1922, Aveling & Porter 5 ton wagon No. 9282, type FGPA, was shipped to Australia and used by the Municipality of Gudegory. It was actually built by Garrett of Leiston as part of the arrangements within the Agricultural & General Engineers' combine, to which both firms belonged at that time. The wagon was returned to England by the late Tom Varley in derelict condition in 1978 and subsequently restored. It now resides at a garden centre near Todmorden, West Yorkshire, where it was pictured in June 2002. (Photograph: Andrew Gibb)

Societies

The *National Traction Engine Trust* (NTET) was formed in 1954 and caters for those with an interest in all types of road steam vehicles. It is the driving force behind the steam vehicle preservation movement and there are many local traction engine clubs affiliated to the organisation as well as several overseas clubs. The NTET can be contacted by writing to John Cook, Dolfarni, Church Lane, Kirkby la Thorpe, Sleaford, Lincolnshire NG34 9NU.

The *Road Locomotive Society* is the 'learned society' for those involved in traction engines and steam wagons. It was founded in 1937. The Society's library is second to none and many aspects of the history of steam wagons, traction engines and their manufacturers can be researched from information held in the Society's files. The Membership Secretary is Donna Boothman, 186 Main Street, Horsley Woodhouse, Derby DE7 6AX.

The *Sentinel Drivers Club* can be reached by writing to Mrs W. Tuxworth, 3 Rayments Bungalows, Wimbish Green, Saffron Walden, Essex CB10 2XL. Website: www.sentinel-waggons.co.uk

For the *Foden Society*, please contact the Secretary at 13 Dudfleet Lane, Horbury, Wakefield, West Yorkshire WF4 5EX. Telephone: 01924 275544. Website: www.thefodensociety.co.uk

The *Leyland Society*. Contact the Secretary: Mike A. Sutcliffe, 'Valley Forge', 213 Castle Hill Road, Totternhoe, Dunstable, Bedfordshire LU6 2DA. Email: sutcliffes@valleyforge.fslife.co.uk

The *Thornycroft Society*. The Secretary is George Johns, 17 Highfield Chase, Basingstoke, Hampshire RG21 1SA. There is also the *Thornycroft Register*, the contact for which is Simon Longden on 01928 733151; website: www.thornycroft.org.uk

A very well restored example of an S4 model by Sentinel of Shrewsbury, pictured at Dorset in 1988. This was one of a pair which initially worked in Scotland – No. 9032 of 1934; the other, No. 9031, is now in the United States, having been shipped there in the early 1960s from Yorkshire.